BOOK ONE

Christmas Impressions

EIGHT FAVORITE CHRISTMAS CAROLS ARRANGED FOR EARLY INTERMEDIATE TO INTERMEDIATE PIANISTS

Catherine Rollin

FOREWORD

One of the most meaningful ways of sharing the joy of the holiday season is through the gift of music. The tradition of playing Christmas carols is one that brings beauty and significance to this special time. It is my wish to bring to pianists this gift of musical celebration through these piano impressions of my favorite Christmas melodies.

Wishing you a joyous holiday season!

CONTENTS

Alfred

Cover Art: Ted Engelbart

It Came Upon the Midnight Clear

Richard S. Willis
Arr. by Catherine Rollin

21
cresc.
mf
26
a tempo
dim. e poco rit.
mp
simile
31
36
rit.
p

Joy to the World

George F. Handel
Arr. by Catherine Rollin

Allegro

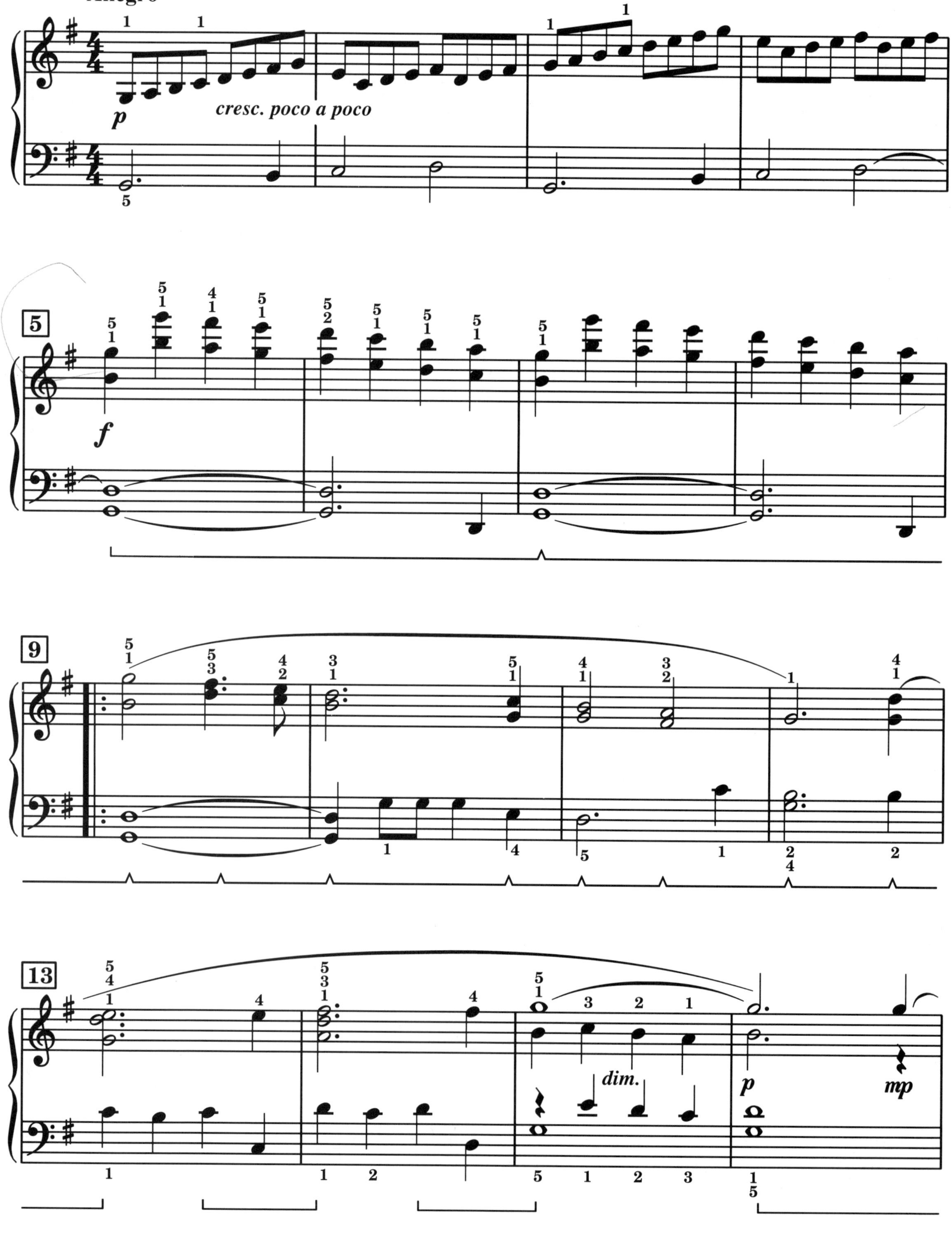

17
p
22
cresc.
26
mf
f
30
cresc.
rit.
ff

What Child Is This?

English
Arr. by Catherine Rollin

Flowing

16
p
mp
20
dim.
24
p
mf
28
dim.

32
mp
f
36
dim. poco a poco
rit.
40
a tempo
8va
p
mp
p
44
a tempo
8va
LH over
poco rit.
dim. e rit.
pp

Silent Night

Franz Grüber
Arr. by Catherine Rollin

A peaceful waltz tempo

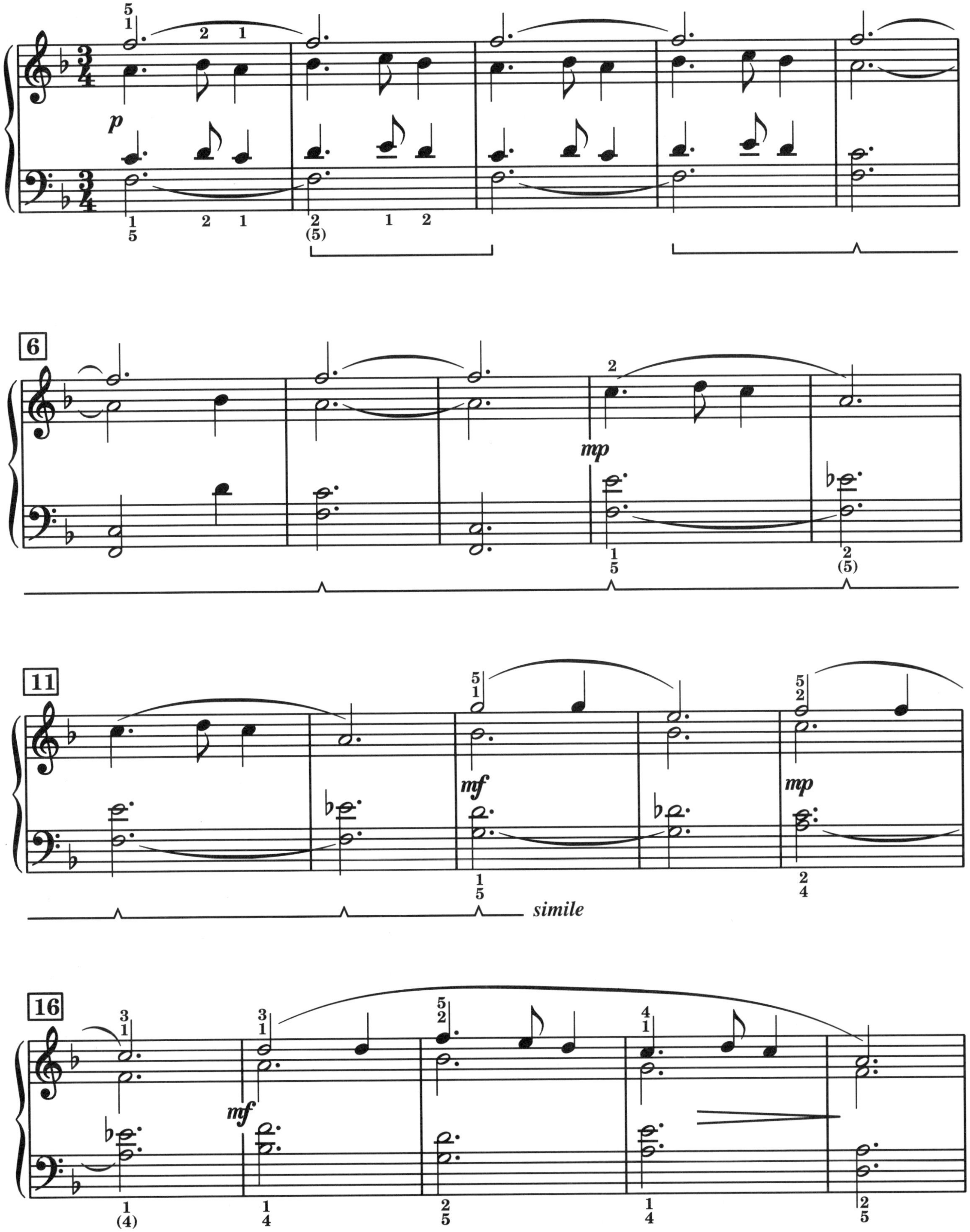

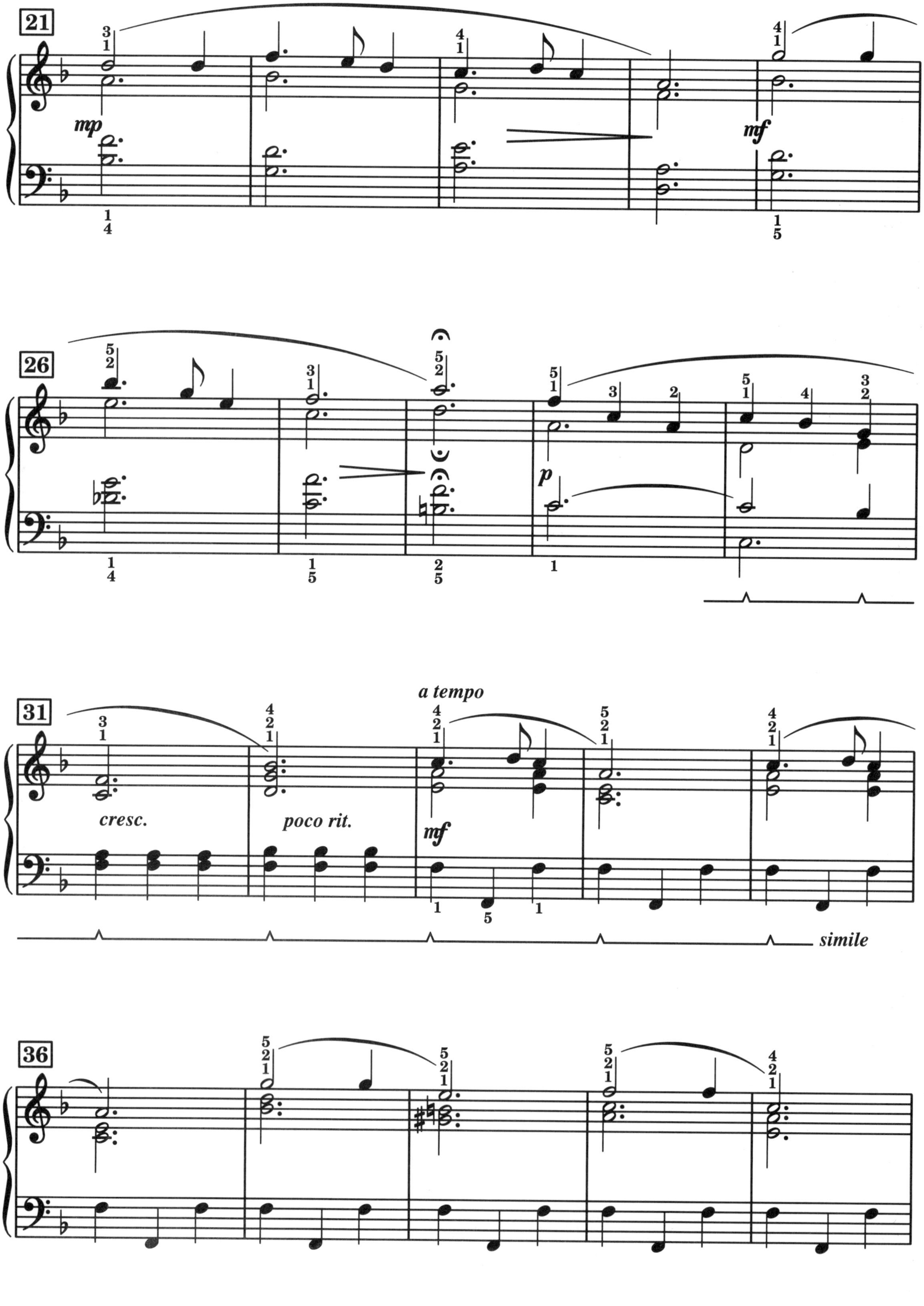
21
mp
mf
26
p
31
cresc.
poco rit.
a tempo
mf
simile
36

41
f
dim.
p
47
mf
cresc. e rit.
f
53
a tempo
mp
rit.
a tempo
p
58
8va
dim.
pp
rit.

Deck the Halls

Cheerfully

Welsh Carol
Arr. by Catherine Rollin

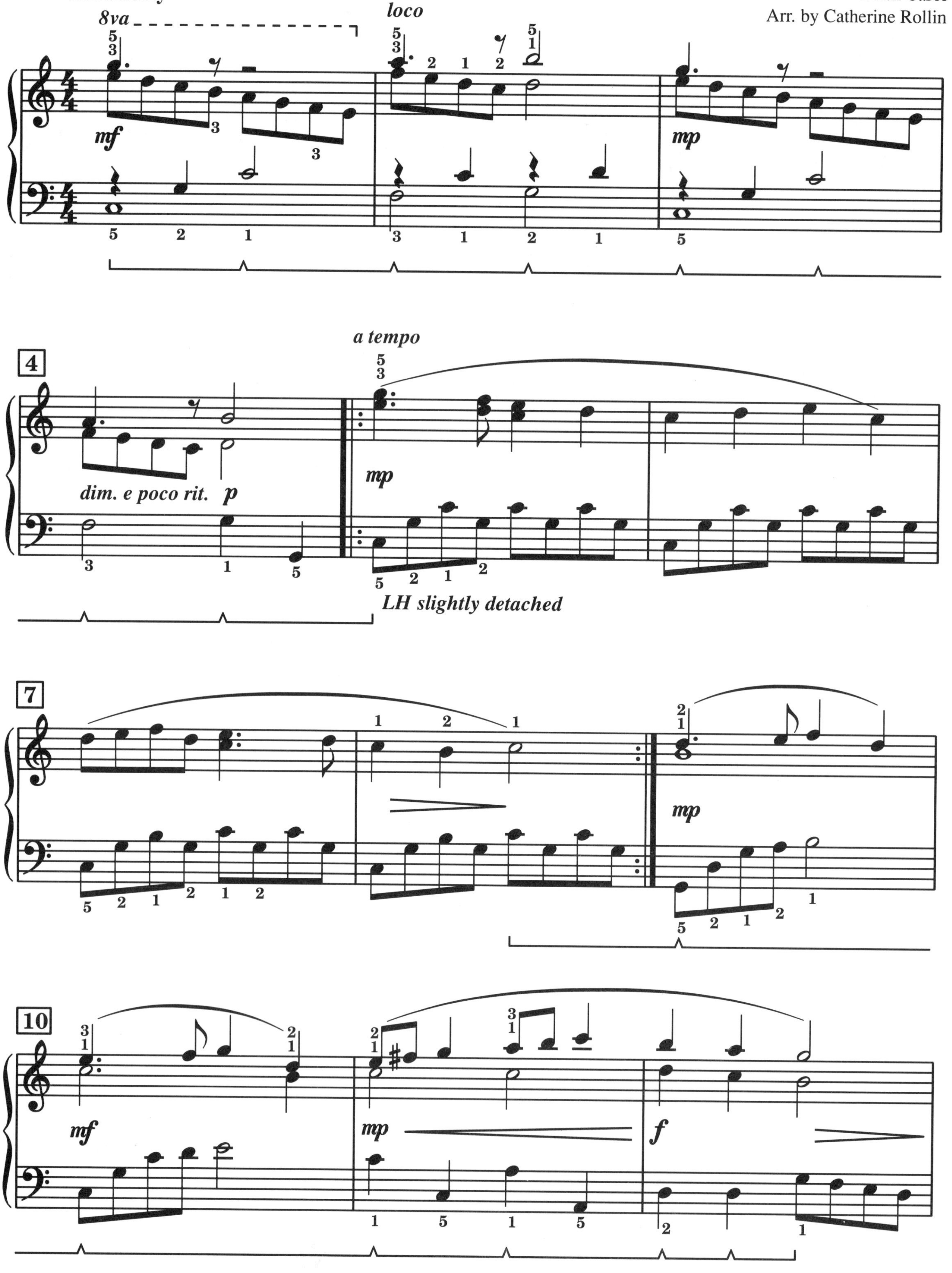

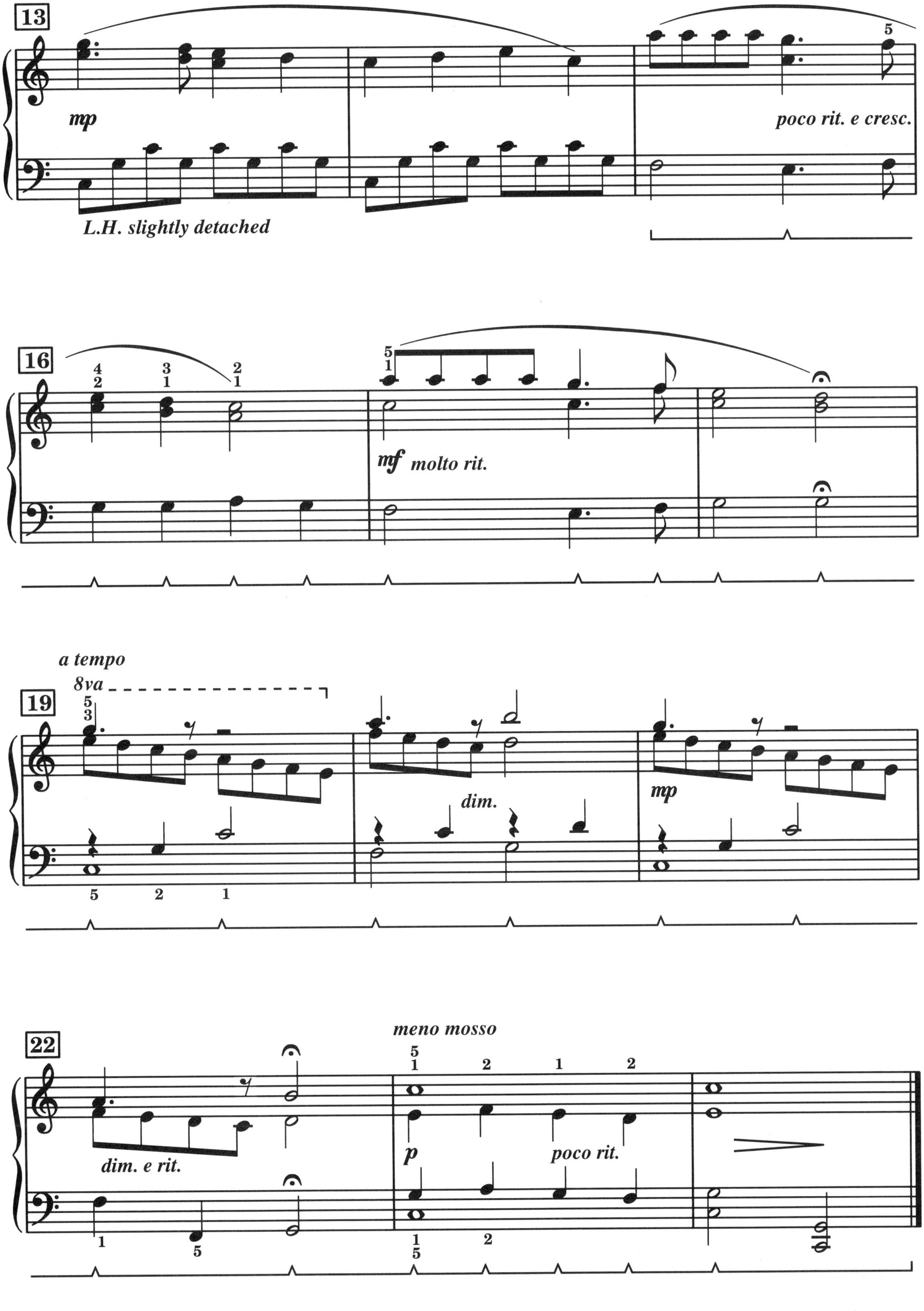
13
mp
L.H. slightly detached
poco rit. e cresc.
16
mf molto rit.
a tempo
8va
19
dim.
mp
22
meno mosso
dim. e rit.
p
poco rit.

Carol of the Bells

M. Leontovich
Arr. by Catherine Rollin

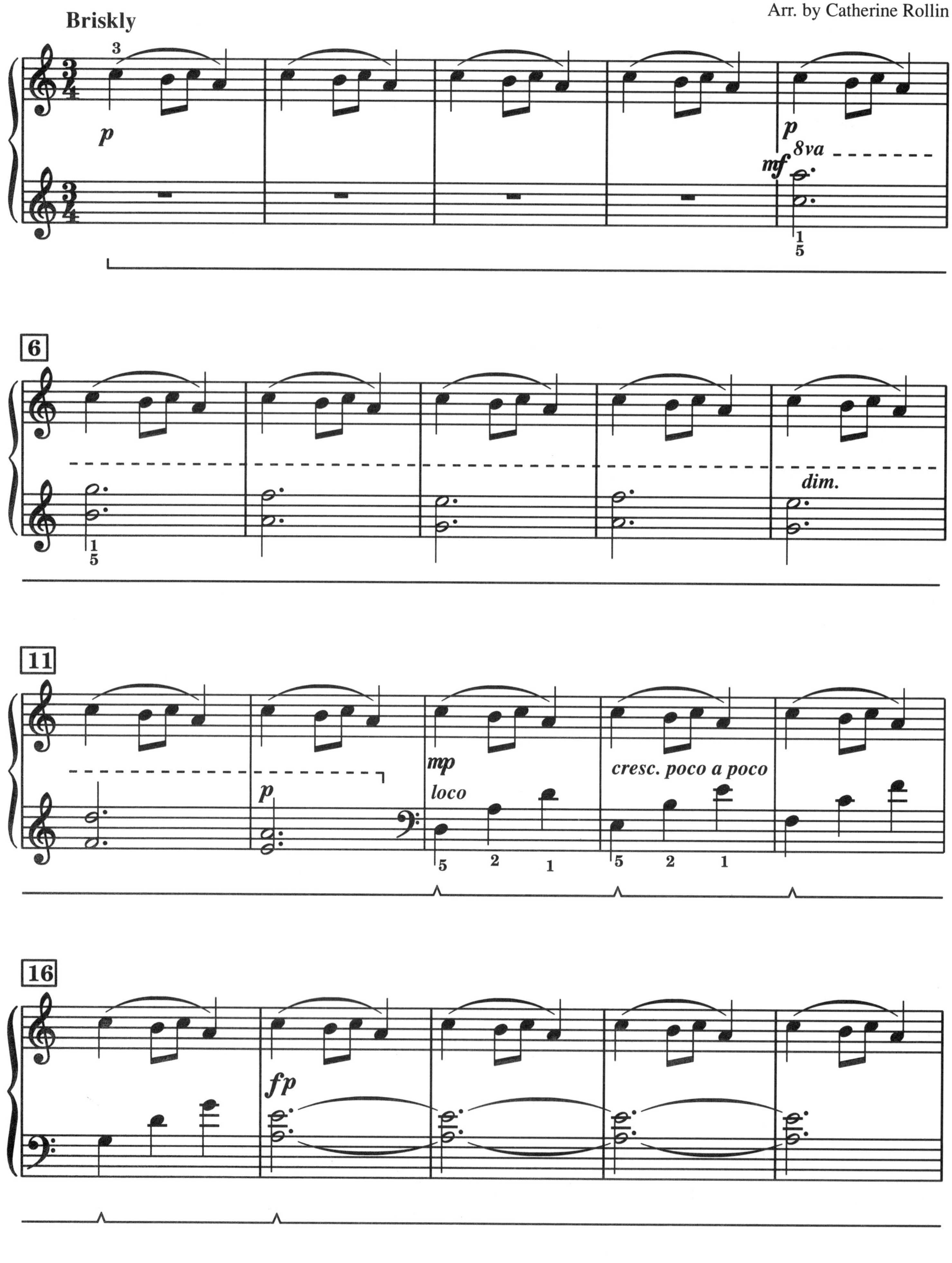

21
mp
mf pp
mp
mf pp
mp
26
mf pp
mp
mf pp
mf
f pp
31
mf
f pp
mf
f pp
mf
36
f pp
f

41
mp
mp
45
p
f
dim.
mp
50
p
p
8va
f
55

60
8va
p
mf
65
dim.
pp
mp
p
mf
70
pp
mp
p
rit.
dim.
mf
75
a tempo
p
dim. e molto rit.
pp
p
mp
mp

Angels We Have Heard on High

French Carol
Arr. by Catherine Rollin

15
mp
19
mf
23
27
f
mp
dim.
p

31
mp
p
simile
35
mp
p
39
mp
42

45
mf
48
poco rit.
a tempo
51
f
mp
cresc. poco a poco
54
rit.
ff
LH over

O Little Town of Bethlehem

Moderate and tenderly

Lewis H. Redner
Arr. by Catherine Rollin

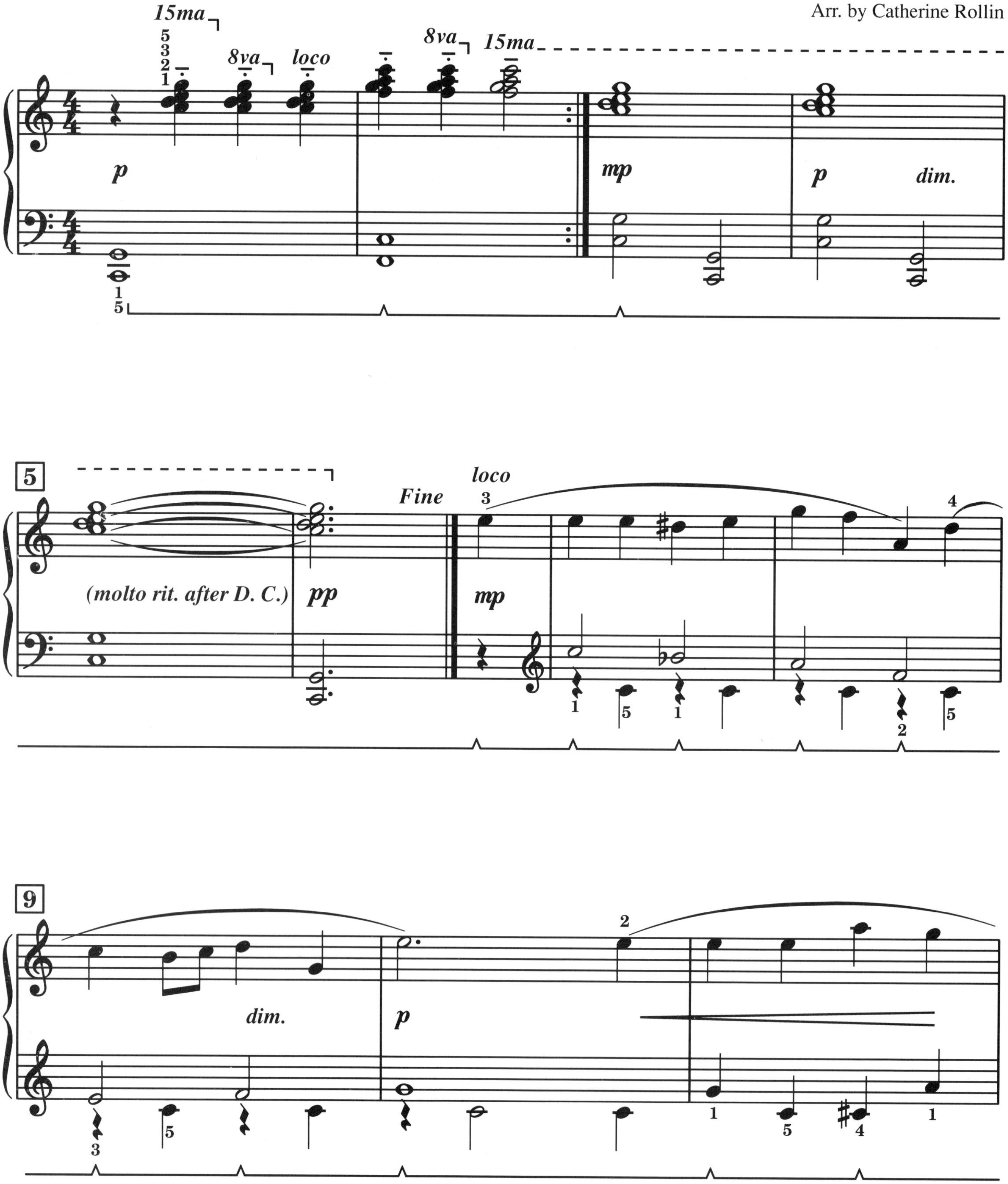

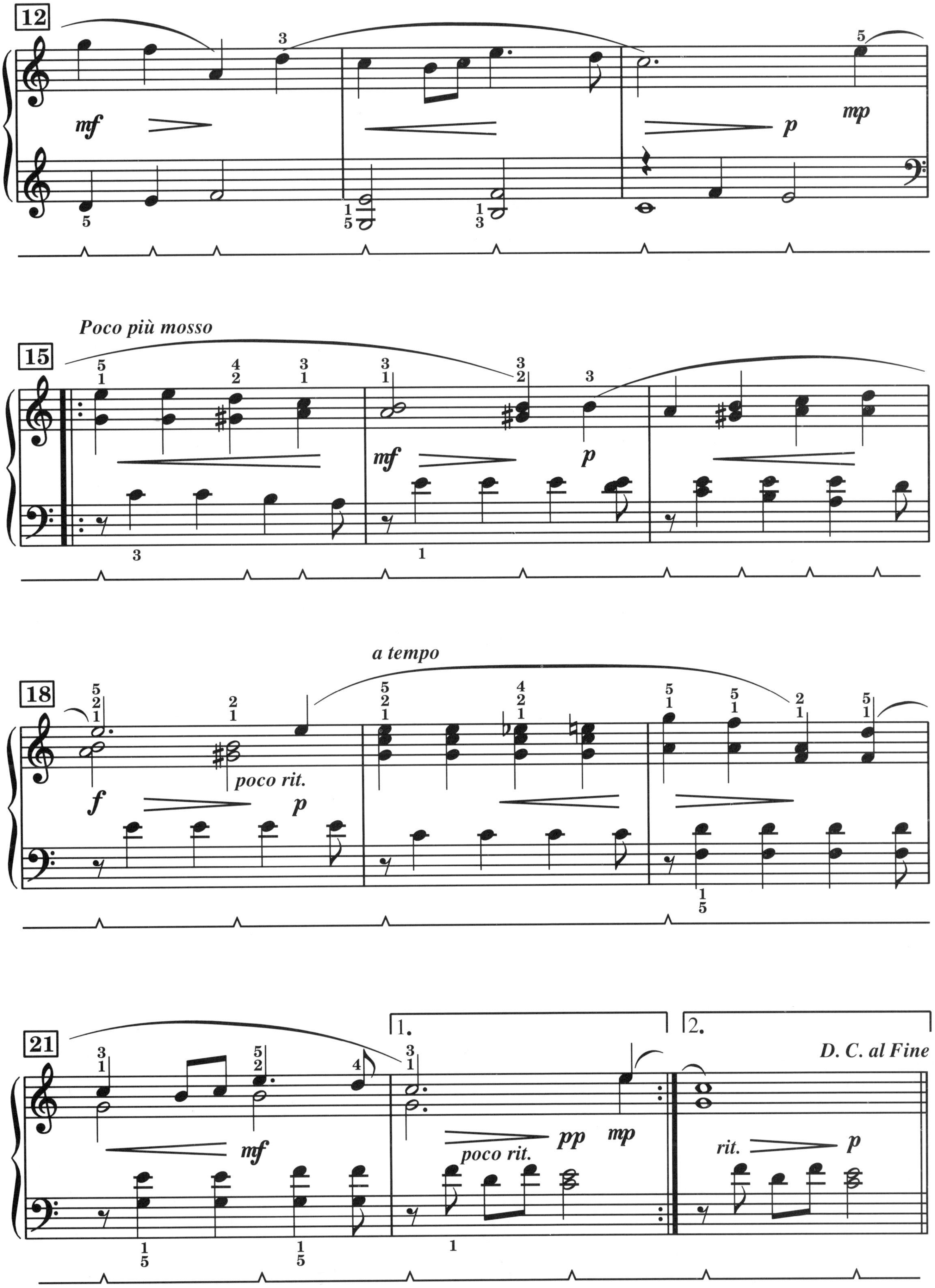
12
mf
p
mp
Poco più mosso
15
mf
p
18
a tempo
f
poco rit.
p
21
mf
1.
2.
D. C. al Fine
poco rit.
pp
mp
rit.
p

BIOGRAPHY

Catherine Rollin, composer, pianist and teacher, earned a B.M.A. degree with distinction from the University of Michigan and a M.M. degree from Oakland University. She is an active teacher and was voted "Teacher of the Year" in 1987 by her colleagues of the Detroit Musicians League. In addition to writing music specifically for piano students, Catherine has written concert works for piano, violin and voice. She has been commissioned by *Clavier* magazine, the Music Teachers National Association and the Michigan Music Teachers Association. Her versatility with both serious and pop music has enabled her to work in commercial music. Over 20 commercials have aired on radio and television using music written, performed and produced by Catherine.

Of all her composing, however, it is Catherine's writing for students that she finds the most gratifying. "When students play and learn from my music, I feel that I am contributing to their musical development. For me this is very rewarding and a special privilege."

Although she is a dedicated piano teacher, Catherine confesses that in the summer she likes to be outdoors as much as her piano students. She is an avid swimmer, jogger and gardener. A Detroit native, she currently lives with her husband in Bloomfield Hills, Michigan.